Thief

Thief

poems
Jennifer Stewart Miller

GRAYSON BOOKS
West Hartford, Connecticut
www.graysonbooks.com

For my mother and father

Late August night—
listening to crickets
thinking of fireflies

Contents

1

My Dead   13
Silversides   14
Baby Doc & the Green Crab   15
On Seeing   16
Cleaning the Night Basement   17
Gutted   19
Too   20
Knees   21
Admission   22
Happy   24
Poetry Is Stolen Fruit   25
Dumped in swampy ground, axles up   26

2

Sister Art   29
Landscape with Crooked-Legged Dog   30
Interior with Black Squirrel   31
Blizzard Aubade   33
Great Aunt Marie Speaks Her Only Epitaph   34
A Gift   35
Treatment   36
Because the pear tree   37
Train   38
Due Date   39
Grackle   40
Cabbage White Butterfly   41
March   42
Safekeeping   44

3

Arrival   49
Waiting   50
e.e. cummings' desk   51
My Niece's Father   53
After Hearing How You Mistook My Words   54
Fledging   55

Thirsty Birds   57
How to Fletch Your Own Arrow   59
By the San Francisco Airport Marriott the Morning After a
        Guardianship Hearing   60
The Sun Was Going Down   61
At the Mortuary   62
Under the Apple Tree   63

4

The End   67
Happy   68
Poems I Probably Won't Write About My Stepfather   69
I Don't Want to Go Up in Smoke   70
Slack Tide   71
To the Dead Striped Bass Swimming in Sunset   72
How to Convince Your Mother to Give Up the Farm   73
Dual Diagnosis   74
Emerge   75
Walking Woman   76
Lines Written on a Loon's Skull   79
This poem has a highway in it   81
Thief   82
Leave It   83

Notes   84
About the Author   85
Acknowledgments   86

1

My Dead

My dead
aren't good on their feet.

My dead slip from ladders,
tumble down stairs, reach

for handles and miss.
Maybe they're house painters or

old sea captains. Maybe, à la
Ahab, they lack a leg.

I thought I could make it,
my father said.

The search for more time.
The white whale

finding us instead.
The surprise.

An untied lace. A protruding
thought on a stair's tread.

Have you tried lifting
a dead person off the floor?

Go ahead—wrap a dead arm
around your neck.

Maybe your dead
are kinder. But mine—

they won't look you
in the eye. Won't

say sorry or
bare their hearts.

They won't even admit
how heavy they are.

Silversides

Driving to pick the kids up at school,
I try to recall the name of this minnow—
my sister would know it, she's the one
with the net for details, quicksilver flashes
in the shallows, the state capitols and birds
in car games we played on long drives.
As for me—spare me the details,
let the minnows go.
She calls me on the phone again,

says she tries to sleep but only dozes—
jerks awake all night. It's the voodoo,
she says, the pins sticking in all over her—
she says she found the doll the nurses made.
And they stole the keys to her car,
dumped in all this filth—fish heads
and stinking soil, her car is crawling.
Vines jungling: she dozes, she wakes—
they squeeze their way around her neck.

I want instead to remember summers
when she and I were small—long days
on the town beach, the drone
of boat engines, how we would scoop up
salt water in our blue and yellow pails,
slosh it up the sand, and watch the minnows
flop about, flash their little lightning—
then we plopped them into a big bucket
and left them to swim around for the afternoon.
Did we let them go in time?
Here they are, swimming up in my throat.

Baby Doc & the Green Crab

The NYT today says Haiti's Baby Doc
Duvalier is dead. So that's that—

another brutal dictator escapes without
paying his tab. It's almost dusk

as a cloud a little darker than the others
leans down to kiss the grey sea.

I'm glad to be reminded of tenderness,
even by a cloud. Though I didn't say this

out loud, a Zen-master gull
floating nearby gives me the eye,

&, as if delivering a newspaper, a wave
tosses a one-armed green crab at my feet—

upside down on the sand, legs scrabbling.
I flip it right-side up. The crab

is not grateful—menaces me with its only claw,
which is ragged & broken, part

of a pincer snapped off. It won't let me
nudge it closer to the water,

furiously churns backside down into damp sand,
until only two stalk-eyes

stare at me accusingly—like tiny heads
impaled on buried pikes.

On Seeing

Genus Planaria—*tiny flatworms found
under rocks in streams and ponds*

Sunlight glints off two upside-down shiny
tin trash can lids and off the water that fills
and fills them from a garden hose:
the water shivers in these silvery pools.

My mother, cross-legged, hunches over the lids,
recording what her flatworms are doing.
For this experiment, she's chopped off
their heads—killed them I fear—*No, no,*
she explains, *their heads grow back—
you can even split them in half.* Sunlight
flashes too brightly off the water, off
the new metal, and she says, *Look, do you see
how they're turning away, how they don't need
eyes to see the sun?*

And this is the world, always, my whole life,
this brightness: *Look, Mom, no eyes!
I know where the sun is.* But now I see
where they were going all along—their sun
is under rocks—it's the dark that shines.

Cleaning the Night Basement

On a ledge in the back
          room   I can
dimly make out

   a nest made of decaying
fur and grey sticks—big like
          a squirrel's nest   I don't

   want to see   any
of this   but   a rat
          fat   like an opossum

uncurls and
          casually   leaps down
brushes past

my stiff legs and
morphs into a
          raccoon   which squats

   and stares through its mask—
          something
gnaws at me   and I squeeze

through a little hole
   my mother's boyfriend
               and I

               lie on
a twin bed in her room
watching   the only TV—

He slides his big
hand
          down

          under the waistband
of my pajamas
          his fingers

insinuate their way
  under   the elastic
        of my

        underpants
and
        stroke my   newish

little mammal patch.
              He
        pauses

bites back
        most of
  a moan

  withdraws his
             hand—
but not

        the rat
and not
        its doppelganger

the raccoon
    with its   sorry
        little hands.

Gutted

At the pig farm next door,
our neighbors are burning leaves—

the smoke smell masks the pig stink,
and rises with us as we climb the hill

behind their house. We run ahead
of our parents, my little sister and I,

into the circus-colored trees. Close by,
a crow caws, and off in the distance,

a pack of dogs bays. We kick along,
the shuush shush shuush of leaves

underfoot, we're nearly home when
we see her, a doe—lying there,

cornered by barbed wire, invisible
in the fiery leaves until the eyes

adjust. Alive, her belly
a jumble of guts.

The dogs. Ears alert,
she looks at us, big eyes

with nothing to hide except
why she won't close them.

Too

My sister was beautiful—

beautiful as a clean sheet snapping and dancing
on a tight line in a brisk wind,

beautiful as a blonde beach shimmering with heat
as it spills into a hazel sea on a summer day.

When I was thirteen
and she was eleven,

I overheard my mother worrying
that my sister would be too beautiful.

Jealousy stung, welted my heart.
I was adored—but enough

wasn't enough. First born,
I wanted to be first in everything.

Now she and I are getting older.
But I still compare—do I look

younger than she does? Her life
has been hard. Over and over

she tries. These days,
her only daughter—thirteen,

blonde and lovely—
lives with me.

Snow is falling today.
Too beautiful.

Knees

Tomorrow, my father gets his foot
cut off—too much pain for too long—
time for another divorce.

81 now, for years he declared
he was too old for this.
Maybe he was too young—

what a shiver, sickness,
wheelchairs, walkers,
canes. There's been talk

of complications,
of a cut above the knee—
like the hem on a sexy skirt.

But he will insist, he says,
on below the knee. March—
a bit of snow clings

to the ground, but in his garden
he's planted spinach already.
By my front steps this morning,

the hyacinths just beginning
to bulge out of the ground
remind me of knees—

how green and incipient
we can always be.
Below the knee—

all the things
he has done,
has not done,

could do,
can still do,
on his knees.

Admission

That first time, 20 years ago,
        we didn't know

what was wrong as J sank
        into her tar-pit—

words and limbs thick
        and slurred, heart rate

slowed. What a cold
        December: fired from her job,

stacks of parking tickets
        and bills. No insurance.

Don't parents know
        who to ask, what

to do? No. On New Year's Eve,
        the E.R. is the last,

the only place for us
        to go. Hours of

waiting. Forms to fill out,
        questions, examinations, tests—

do you love
        your sister? Explanations,

qualifications, more questions,
        more waiting waiting.

Until the doctor says, *Admit.*
        With a nervous laugh,

my sister asks, *Can I borrow*
        your underwear? We cried

laughing—and was I
    ever closer to her?

Happy

After the first psych ward and treatment,
after cigarette burns on mattresses, after
she was jailed, and her boyfriend

punched her, after one of them drove
my mother's truck right into the ocean—
good news! A baby.

Are you happy for me?
Can't you just be happy for me?
Are you coming to my baby shower?

I, with my three children, knew exactly
what she wanted. And I wanted
for everything not to happen.

How many times already
had her blazing HazMat train car
roared through our peaceful little towns?

She was doing better, she said, she was
taking her meds. Were we stuck in the past?
Maybe we were still burning,

smoking a little. As was she—hadn't
we taken her to the psych ward
on New Year's Eve? New Year's Eve!

She was dying to celebrate, I guess.
Holidays, it turns out, are very important—
they're the days you prove your life

is normal—you have family, they
love you, they want you around. True—
things had been tranquil for a few months,

and they had a little house. What if I
had had less doubt? Would
a little more happiness have helped?

Poetry Is Stolen Fruit

Sweetest that way   dripping juices
and aphorisms *the best words* I want
peaches but never enough.

Shall I compare thee to love
and porn *I know it when I see it* these
imaginary gardens

with real toads in them. Scratch that
Moore said *I too dislike it* but didn't.
No as in why. As in how

*a summer's day must ride on
its own melting.* Like little animals
trapped inside *this poor body*

*composed of one hundred bones
and nine openings* imaginary
toads with real gardens in them.

How did I get here as I
write it I itch to pilfer it. Bicker
bitch covet I sleep with it

blackberry nights slow striptease
of days I want to cheat on my love my
life with it   peaches peaches.

Dumped in swampy ground, axles up,

the rusted-out truck is beginning to sink in,
like how old age starts to grip. My mother doesn't like
to drive at night; she clutches the wheel and talks about
close calls. After my son's graduation, he drives off.

We, too, go our separate ways, wanting to be home
before dark. I stop at the park—there are barriers now;
kids don't sneak up here anymore to light fires,
and kiss, and melt car parts and beer bottles,

and you can't just drive your wreck off
the Sprain Brook Parkway and abandon it in the forest
to founder beside open-mouthed washing machines.

Birds flit in and out of shadows; old stone walls
wander off into the trees. After it was junked, the truck
still must have taken years to morph into this—

its cooling fan has burgeoned into a burnt sunflower,
its scrunched front end makes a cubist face,

while out of the Chevy's guts, something like
a T-rex rears its rusty head—a ferocious reminder

of all the undoing to be done, even of the wrecked.

2

Sister Art

1.

An abandoned power station has been transformed
into an art museum—in destruction is creation.

In mist, in mirrors, an artificial sun rises
as my sister enters the room—

    my visitor   my installation.

2.

Sleeping inside the gaping jaws of a monster shark,
my sister dreams of a house with a white picket fence.

A horse made of brass cast to look like driftwood
plods down the middle of the night street

saddled in street light—where is it going?
I want to leave her room but with each step backward

her heartbeat grows louder—
whoomp whoomp whOOMP WHOOMP.

Two halves of a cow, two halves of her calf—
mother and child, the label says. Or sisters.

A bouquet of white light bulbs! My heart
delights me, the way it sees:

the shadow of a word within a word
projected on a wall—*heart heart*—

and these neon colors, how her orange fabric
dazzles against bare trees and snow.

Landscape with Crooked-legged Dog

After Paysage enneigé, *Vincent Van Gogh, 1888*

So you leave winter behind—
the dark, the snow—take a train
south, to sun-drenched Arles,
where there's a brilliance,
a clarity you can't explain

because your tongue
lacks the fine bristles
of a paintbrush, lacks those
hairsbreadth spaces where the light
waits. You need to see this

for yourself—the way the road
through the fields is fringed
with sun-gold stubble poking
through snow, how the earth's
aqua green ochre seeps

through white smudges.
So you leave behind grey
shivering Paris, descend from
the train into a freak snow.
And then you realize

it's not winter that follows you—
or the snow, or the dark—
but the light. No, not the light—
something inside the light that is
faithful and tenacious, like

the crooked-legged dog.
See how she follows
the black-hatted man as he trudges
across the fields towards the blue
town and that one red roof?

Interior with Black Squirrel

A black squirrel sips
the warm water I poured
on a copper bowl of ice—

morning sun
X-rays the squirrel's tail.
The black filaments

billow with light,
what Vermeer was after,
over and over,

the sacred interior.
Not a still life. Not
domestic, this light.

My father's 84th
was last Friday. Restless,
a man of many trespasses,

he's lost a step—in fact
a leg. He scarcely leaves
the house, sits

reading, or relishing
the goings on outside—
squirrels, cardinals.

He's eating when I call—
a Reuben and fries—
and sipping a beer.

One of those
moments, where
do they come from, jazz

playing in the background,
dark outside, his voice
luminous. As if

his many black filaments
are the very reason he catches
so much light.

Blizzard Aubade

All night long, the snowplows plowed up
our shawling dreams—my love,
we were scraped down to the road
and salted to sleep again and again.

What was frozen melted and froze anew,
and still it kept snowing—joys and regrets
piling up, drifting into corners and against
doors. Wind howled at our windows.

Like a woolly mammoth, morning lumbers
toward us. As it was long ago—thick wool
of forgotten eons—we drowse in our
downy burrow, bodies spooned, respiration

slowed. Our history is buried in snow.
What was human is only mammal now.

Great Aunt Marie Speaks Her Only Epitaph

For Marie Bucci, 1908-2005

Every Sunday,
my mother made us go—

not two nickels
to rub together, but still,

we had to dress up,
buy flowers,

and visit the dead.
To honor them,

my mother said.
Every Sunday.

But what about the living?
Death isn't a place

I want to practice going.
One thing I know is,

I don't want
to be buried.

My Henry's ashes—
we took them out

to that golf course
he loved so much,

and shook them out
in a wind.

A Gift

A dirty cardboard box, scotch-taped shut—
grease spots and cigarette smells. On a scrap of paper,
scrawled black slashes, a familiar hand, an unfamiliar
language, but my heart knows it—lurches.

Inside: a rock, a toy golf ball, a CD: *The Essential O'Jays*;
a stained blue t-shirt, a plastic cup. And one
scuffed sneaker: tucked in the heel, a half-eaten packet
of peanut M&M's; in the toes, a crumpled pack of Marlboros.

I replay her message: slurred words, euphoric laughter—
Did you get the box? It's a gift. He won't get away
with it, my Ex—they know now. I'm on fire—everything's
so clear. You'll see. I left it by the back door.

The kitchen falls silent. I close the flaps of the box.
Smoky tendrils of tape curl up—and love's reek.

Treatment

Straight from the locked hospital
I drive her. First, she must check in

at the office—how jovial she is,
as if I'm dropping her off for college,

except she's too old, I can't come in,
and she's not bringing a popcorn popper,

or much besides five packs of Marlboros
and a $1200 prescription she can't pay for.

We joke about it now, how when she
was born, I took one look at her

and wacked her on the head with my bottle—
Welcome home, little sister!

What a blow. Siblings for life.
For her birthday,

I drive back across the Bay
to the rehab house.

We sit in the locked garden,
and go through the motions of

sisterhood and celebration: making
small talk, nibbling bites of—

how merciless the self is—
bittersweet chocolate cake.

Because the pear tree

is as fluffy-white and absurd as a prize poodle,
and thunder clouds sidle into the blue sky like thieves;

because the maple's new leaves are as tiny
and perfect as the hands of a fetus,

and anyone can see that some toucans
lead secret lives as tulips;

because all the shades of green we've named are not
enough, and over and over we sow the seeds,

and peony buds bulge like bellies pregnant
with overdue babies,

while the lawn mower droning in the distance
aspires to be a hive of bees—

in spring, I should know better, but still—
I want to sink down on my knees.

Train

Ambling barefoot and half-dressed along a glass-strewn path beside the train tracks my sister puffs a cigarette—a train thunders past, eyes wide and blank, and then another. She makes it to the station and gets on the next train. Having lain awake all night, she drops to sleep but when she opens her eyes she's stumbling along beside the tracks as another train passes—she glimpses her young daughter on board, face pressed to the window, screaming silently, begging her to catch the train—and then she's on the train and searching from car to car. Glimpsing her daughter, she struggles down the crowded aisle—but my sister is not onboard, she's slumped beside the path, her feet are all cut up, she's too tired to move, and she craves a cigarette. A train is coming and her daughter is on it; as the train brakes, gliding into the station, she runs and makes it to the platform just as the doors are closing. She pries the doors apart and gets on, but she can feel it now, an engine inside her—the train has tunneled into her arteries, it races to the turntable and sling-shots around, speeding through her veins and back to the turntable again, pistons churning, churning. We all watch—daughter sisters mother father brother—we are all small enough to watch, our faces pressed to the glass. She wants to stop the train, but it's too fast, too fast—it hurtles around inside—won't stop won't stop won't won't won't won't

Due Date

I once got so irritated, so impatient
with the inconvenience of yet another trip
to the psych ward to bring J

slippers and sweatpants, underwear
and socks, quarters for the corridor phone—
all the necessities—that I sniped,

You should keep a little bag packed—
as if you were pregnant,
as if it were almost your due date.

Today I call—she's in another dive motel,
says the coffee pot is covered in shit
and roaches are crawling out of the wallpaper

and over her arms. How ordinary
such calls are now—first stop psych ward,
then it's off to the dual diagnosis house.

This time, though, J isn't
just across the Bay—I've moved east,
to the other side of the country,

from where I can finally see. She is
pregnant, so terribly pregnant, only
it's she who keeps trying to be born.

Grackle

Even ugly birds love bird baths—
bruise black, they swoop in,
jockey on branches, on the feeder,
raucous as a crowd of teenagers,

hard-eyed all. The flock flies off.
But one male loiters, surveys the yard,
hops into the undersized bowl—beak
and throat stretch up, wings

shatter water into sun droplets,
the wet black glints iridescent purple
and the one eye's golden—
he cocks his head—that eye says

there's a bird inside
the bird he is.

Cabbage White Butterfly

As it sips from even our tiniest
flowers   ordinary life is like
the common Cabbage White—

easy to overlook. After J's
regular visit to the psychiatrist
we share another picnic at the park.

Daughter in her lap   she offers me
her envelope of receipts. Eyes
like a stray cat   too little sleep

or something else? Her blue-eyed
husband beats her   and I do and don't
believe her   the stories she tells.

She refuses to leave him though.
As I check her penciled calculations
and dole out this month's paltry cash—

I don't dare give her more—J
untangles the child's long
blonde hair. She brushes and brushes

and divides it into two neat ponytails.
My niece wears white sandals
pink leggings   and an immaculate

white top. My sister wipes a smudge
of chocolate off the child's cheek.
A lock of hair has escaped—J

sweeps it back   and as her daughter
tries to wriggle out of her lap   pins
the stray hair with a butterfly clip.

March

First light. From far across
the foggy, half-frozen lake,
the sound of geese—all night,

their distant, gathering cries
soothed me back to sleep.
Something under the ice.

Around the lake—
Norway spruce, blue spruce,
white pine.

I wish my father
could hear the geese, but he
is miles away.

More and more he sleeps—
dozes in his chair, naps long hours,
body sprawled across his bed.

Flesh has melted off his body
like ice off the lake. Every embrace
is down to the bone.

Along the shore, a yacht club
without any yachts,
snow drifted up

against the doors, as in
a childhood storm.
When he was a kid,

my father found
a Colt pistol
hidden in the ruins of a barn—

old enough to have been used
in the Civil War, though he
was too young

to think of that.
Swathed in fog, the geese,
their distant, gathering cries.

Last night, I cracked
the storm window open.
Now I open it wide—

a stream or a spring
burbles away unseen.
My father still frets

about that gun,
what it might have been worth,
how he used it

to crack some nuts.
I think of how he holstered it
and has carried it all his life—

the possibilities, how things
might have been different.
In a patch of open water,

one goose
swims round and round.

Safekeeping

In 2012 in Timbuktu,
under the burning eyes
of barbarians,

the guardians of books
carefully wrapped
the ancient manuscripts

in sackcloth,
and smuggled them out
in canoes, cars, donkey carts.

They hid them in bunkers,
and won't be back to fetch them
anytime soon.

A girl, too, is a book
written in an ancient language
of primeval letters

that tell a version
of her mother's history,
and her father's,

and the living world's.
Please, my sister says,
please. From the half-way

house, she calls and calls.
The child
is hiding in the bushes

from her father's
friends. Of all good things
J loves

on this earth, her daughter
comes first, but now
she pleads—

wants to send her
three thousand miles
to me.

3

Arrival

At JFK airport   I glimpse long blonde hair
my niece walks by   and I call

her name. I've made room for her   cleaned out
my daughter's dresser and closet   emptied

the desk   found her a chair. A blue
hyacinth perfumes the chilly room. I hang

a sleeveless dress in the closet   as she
arranges photos of her dog and her mom

by the bed. How long will I be filling in—
playing mother   second violin? Am I

only clay in consequence's hands   or am I
the potter? Thirteen   how shaped she is

already   a girl thrown on what wheel—
too late for more than love's glaze, I fear.

Waiting

Morning blows right in—wind whips up rain,
lights flicker and steady themselves. The dog

dozes, the furnace can't stop blowing. Outside,
wind rises—a storm door bangs open and shut,

and the iron peacock rocks on its stone pivot.
The dog twitches, runs in her dreams—I too

go far, travel nowhere in buffets of wind,
gusts of *something must be done.* When will

the guardianship papers come? I must remember this—
my house was built to take these gusts, it's a hive

inside, with rooms of honey. This is what it means
to be built by someone else—to wait, to withstand,

to breathe like old windows while a child
in a sea-green room is rocked in her dreams.

e.e. cummings' desk

looks more like a dresser:
solid mahogany, one big drawer on top,
below, a cupboard. The drawer

flips down to make the desk—
a secret you can write on,
an inch thick. We are allowed

to touch. Last night, I was reading
Cheever's biography of the man—
now his dog weighs on my mind.

When Cummings was sixteen, he,
his little sister, and their dog set out across
    a lake in an unsinkable canoe.

      Behind the flip-down drawer
are four little drawers, each with
a golden knob and a poem inside.

And *up so floating many bells down*
    goes the boat. Too far
from shore, brother and sister cling

    to the boxes that had been their seats.

Opening the cupboard is like
stealing a peak into a casket—

      decaying papers and books.

It was the dog's fault the boat tipped.
The panicked dog

tries to scramble out of the water
    on top of the girl—
over and on.   Down

under the water she sinks—
So the boy—
he pushes

the dog's head under
and holds it there—under, under...

Where do we find our words?

It's been years. The cubbyholes
below the four little drawers
have been emptied out.

Solid mahogany. How heavy
it must be. I'm thinking of the dog,
not the dog—

What else could he have done—
Death, the boy.

My Niece's Father

An osprey perches in his usual dead pine beside
the salt river. The dog sniffing along the sand

stirs him off his tree like a spoon stirring
cream into coffee—swirl of wings

in cloudy sky. With a scream   he arcs
over us   eyeing the dog and me.

We mean no harm
but are helpless to explain.

*

He loves his child. No doubt he thinks
he did his best. But he has the stare—

blue-sky   dead-cold eyes   plunging in
over and over is a matter of

survival. What he does is
watch   what he does is

grasp and clutch—
as if she were

a fish.

After Hearing How You Mistook My Words

I'm only your temporary guardian,
I said,

failing to imagine
the terrible, beautiful terrain,

the internal Arizona
of where you live—

you're a girl leaning
      over the edge
        of a canyon,

           eyeing

the vertiginous
       drop.

But we will get there, we
will get there—

don't surefooted mules

plod safely
down and

up every
day by

choosing
each

footfall
carefully?

Fledging

Two great horned owlets
learning to fly—
they struggle into the air,
lumber like jumbo jets
on short hops from pine
to pine. This is how
my father gets about
the house: lunging

from chair to chair.
Most of the day, hunched
on branches, the owlets doze.
Nights, they screech
and screech. Hungry, I think.
No more answering hoots
from nearby oaks.

Maybe their parents
are still feeding them—
maybe they just want
more. These days, no matter
what delicacies we bring,
my father scarcely eats. Skin

like a hatchling, bones
jutting out. He's on his way
to flyweight.
His grandsons' rowdy play,
which used to irritate him—

he watches hungrily now.
I show him grainy photos
of the owlets at dusk, scrunched
next to each other up

in a snag—fierce-eyed,
downy creatures, half-
feathered. He makes a little

sound in his throat, closes
his eyes. Aching
not to fly.

Thirsty Birds

As the dog and I walk up the road,
a yellow-shafted flicker

sips the runoff from a busted sprinkler—
dips in, tips back, dips in, tips back—

its long beak and red-dabbed head
raise and lower like one of those

oil well pumps, also known as thirsty birds,
I last saw years ago, out near LAX.

I tug the dog to a stop
and let the flicker slake its thirst.

I've never seen one drink.
Beak pointed skyward, the bird pauses.

It's early, it's summer, it's
going to be another scorcher.

You don't have to believe,
to think there's something about

the flicker's up-stretched profile
that's like a shaft of sunlight

piercing an old church.
Just this once, I'm glad

for a broken sprinkler head—
for the bird, for the water

spilling down the road.
I could never quite love L.A.,

but those were good years—
when the children were young,

when we could still afford
to be prodigal with our time.

How to Fletch Your Own Arrow

Steal the sunbird's plumage and sheen—
how the sun anatomizes

emerald green. Appropriate
iridescence and gleam; add

a slice of metallic blue from the throat.
Steal a few verbs—

forage, flit, hover, probe.
Savor their fruit.

Think decurved beak, think
of the nectar it swallows and sings.

Your appendages? These
are not arms, but wings.

Pluck three flight feathers
and lay their quills

along the shaft. At top
and bottom, wrap them fast with

a bit of sinew,
then glue each quill down.

Trim them with scissors,
tight and sweet. Now

you are fletched, now
you are arrow.

By the San Francisco Airport Marriott the Morning After a Guardianship Hearing

For now, the child may remain with me.
On mudflats, birds fly up in sudden sentences,

abruptly land. Sun struggles in clouds. Far off,
a bridge, shrouded in where we came from, looms.

Two terns rise up as one, then fly apart, as will
my sister and her child again this afternoon.

Mired in mud, a half-moon of a truck tire offers
a little horizon—that's all we have. I chose,

so I must choose. It's a choreography of take offs
and landings: depart one world, arrive in another.

But the choices keep coming. Straying
into my sister's eyes, I'm in a bad part of town—

I lock my doors, and drive through quickly.
In these derelict lots beside the Bay, green

isn't personal, it's Spring—lush grasses,
and one California poppy in exuberant bloom.

The Sun Was Going Down

The trees were bare.
The crows came—and congregated in the trees.

Though there wasn't any wind,
they fluttered on the branches.

The cold gnawed at them.
They crowded together.

Night crept in. It crept in
through the cracks of light left in the trees.

They grew quiet, straining to hear.
It wouldn't make a sound.

They knew this.

At the Mortuary

The face is his, yet not his own.
A cloud of snowy hair, blue eyes closed.
My father is stone.

Last I saw him, time was running out—
I thought I knew. Deliberately, I kissed
this cheek—his, but not his. The room

is cold and quiet. He wears his
sky-blue sweatshirt. His ears are bruised.
My father is stone, my stone father—

eyebrows scraggily lichens, smile lines
chiseled around his mouth, which is
his and yet not. No coffin, just

a metal gurney and white blanket—he loved
Eliot's lines: *Let us go then, you and I…*
but this father is stone, he remembers

nothing. His heat has cooled—
marble lips seal a rock tongue.
Stone. This stone is my father.
I do not know him. But the face is his.

Under the Apple Tree

For E.A.S.

Praise fall and these withering leaves.
Praise grief, for the love it's made of, those bees—

how they hummed, how they brought us fruit.
Praise the last days, the last apples dangling on the tree.

Praise the fallen fruit, and bruise and decay—
for the seeds they nourish, the mouths they feed.

Praise the ants reconnoitering loss—
apples cracked open in the grass.

4

The End

I keep coming back to how my mother
left my stepfather

at Rutland Regional Medical Center
to hurry off to the bank in Granville—

thinking she could still add her name
to some account or other by

bringing in a few shaky words he'd
scribbled on a scrap of paper.

And that was that.
After all the grand passion—

just an old married couple
trying to sort things out.

Not giving a thought
to last words.

Who's to say this isn't
how it's supposed to be,

death bustling in like a veteran nurse
come to give a toddler a shot—

rub a little antiseptic, hide
the needle, *Hey*

look at the pink elephant!

Happy

In a grubby motel in downtown Oakland,
my sister combusts again.

And again, the fire trucks arrive,
and again, and every time,

for twenty-something years,
she survives, she gets back up—

like a prize fighter in the movies
who gets beaten to such a swollen,

bloody pulp that even his opponent
can't bear to punch him anymore.

For a while, things always go so well.
Like a fire hydrant popped open

hope gushes out.
But however much you adore

your child, when you're this
flammable, it's just a matter of time.

As for me, I worry that some bright
blue morning, I'll answer the door

and J's Ex will smile at me
with his gun. *A child for a child*,

he'll say. Still—dear reader, here's
a happy ending, if that's

what you want: love,
three thousand miles apart.

Poems I Probably Won't Write About My Stepfather

On Holding the Phone to Your Ear the Night Before
    You Die So Your Half-Sister Can Read You a Poem

On Missing Your Last Breath Because I Had to Stop for Gas

Poem in Which My Mother Reminisces with the Funeral Director
    About Meeting Him When He Was a Little Kid

How to Choose the Right Locally-Sourced Wooden Urn
    for a Former Forester

On First Walking into the Forbidden Sanctum of
    Your Office, AKA, the Junk Room

On Reading Letters in Which You Pour Your Heart Out
    to Your Estranged Boys

Poem in Which I Hide the Scissored Pictures of Sexy Women
    from My Mother

On Boxing Up Your Boy Scout Badges and the Many Clippings
    Extolling Achievements I Wish I'd Known About

On Finding a Heartbroken Letter from Your 2nd Wife

Your Two Youngest Boys Were Gorgeous Toddlers
    and I'm Sad for All of Us

Thinking About Who Might Want Your Guns

Pyre: 12 Garbage Bags of Lectures and Other Papers Return
    to Earth and Sky on a Frigid Windy Day

What to Do with All the Cowboy Hats

On Shipping You to Your Children by First Class Mail

Wondering Why You Never Let My Mother
    Drive Your Pickup Truck

I Don't Want to Go Up in Smoke

Not the way we do it—
a button that's pushed,

the coffin's unctuous glide
into the furnace's whoosh.

I don't want to go up
in smoke,

unless it's Beowulf style—
billowing into sky,

massive pyre wreaking havoc
in the hot bone-house.

I don't want to be
urned or coffee-canned,

I don't want to be
dispersed—

Mound me in earth.

See below:
I want everything,

plus inscription and stone—
femurs & tibiae,

radii & ulnae,
vertebrae, scapulae,

mandible & skull.
All 56 phalanges

of fingers and toes.
I love

the idea
of bones.

Slack Tide

It's that time in September
when summer   a swan
about to head south
glides in for a perfect landing
sky blue   air brisk.
Out in the bay   if you launched
paper boats they wouldn't float off
would just bob around you.
Slack tide here too
last child off to college
plunging in like a black Lab
splashing after a duck.
The house is quiet and clean
like an empty vase.
I should be celebrating
or weeping or oscillating
in between   I feel
the tug   but upstairs
my sister's child sleeps.
Two more years   at least
of a species of motherhood.
If there's fault it isn't hers
she's a lovely girl. My sister keeps
trying   she's finished rehab again
the two of them talk on the phone.
But the moon inside—

To the Dead Striped Bass Swimming in Sunset

Swim on, beached beauty, agog
in the chilly marsh, aglow without
scales or skin. May the jut
of your jaw, your eyeless eyes,
guide you back to the sea. May
your body—filleted of flesh—
follow so lightly. Long, supple
golden spine. Ribs vaulted with
air and light. Moony-white tail.
Even the waves lap you a prayer—
undulate, undulate. Striped bass—
gather up my newly dead, school
with them, show them the way
out of the still-dead April grass.

How to Convince Your Mother
to Give Up the Farm

We'll pack up your two hundred acres, your thirty-odd years
of home—blue birds in the nest box by the pond, the voracious
gaze of the fox, flocks of wild turkeys, the satellite-dish ears
of deer outside windows at dawn. Delicates will be swathed:
memories hanging like icicles from eaves; spider webs in fog;

horses snorting in winter, the plush of muzzles leaning from stalls.
We'll press into paper spring grass in pastures, and wildflowers—
bloodroot, hepatica, dogtooth violets. We'll freeze strawberries,
blueberries, blackberries. The garden can be put up
in jars. We'll shrink-wrap the idea of Hubbard squashes,

how they burgeon from manure piles with such giant dreams. Autumn
leaves—maple, beech, birch—can be dried into fiery seasonings;
friends and neighbors can be smoked like hams—farmers, farriers,
vets, professors, priests. Pancake breakfasts at sugar houses
can be ordered for take-out. We'll ferment the juiciest gossip

into sparkling wine, bubble wrap the last three chickens, the last
two cats, and also the skunks and bad luck—frozen pipes, cracked
bones. Ambulances. Mud, shit, sweat, drought. In sickness
and in health. We'll exhume the border collie struck dumb
by a car. Swaddle the arthritic ewes, the burnt bones

of the ram, stone-heaped graves of mare and ancient racehorse.
We'll digitize crickets, cicadas, and silence. Furl up the poster
of farm: sagging fences, slapdash outbuildings, the long,
trampled scarf of a drive. As for the cauldron of night sky
roiling with stars—we'll roll it up like a carpet.

Dual Diagnosis

For J.M.

And you too shall stand tall,
you who keep falling down.

And you too shall be esteemed,
you who've begged shoeless in the street.

And you too shall jingle your keys,
you who've been locked up.

And you too shall have lovely white teeth,
you who've lit the flame under the pipe.

And you too shall be welcomed by your family,
you who've been shunned.

And you too shall find the fight's been called,
you who keep getting back up.

Emerge

After the tree-toppling blasts
of three late nor'easters, who

doesn't feel it—earth's
tilt, surge of greengreengreen,

thrust of jewels out of
dirt, hyacinth, tulip.

Who can sleep,
birds chortling their

inside-out,
upside-down dirge—

they wake me, wake
the sun. Out on the lawn—

robins hunting worms,
buried things.

My father does not emerge,
does not sing. Waits

on the piano in his
mini-Grecian urn. I unscrew

the lid—his first spring
dead—tip the urn, grit

of his bones, let
a little sun in.

Walking Woman

Giacometti's *Walking*
Woman is a headless lesson,
bronzed and archetypal—

take something, or
everything, away from this woman,
and still, she walks on.

Once, she had a head
But Giacometti chopped it off—
which I can't help but feel

ambivalent about. Eyeing
this lissome female form,
I can imagine why a head

might have seemed
a distraction. And yet,
there's something about a head...

In a darkened room, a video plays
in which blind people paint
self-portraits on huge sheets

of paper rolled out on the floor.
And the first thing they each do
is give themselves a head.

Squirting black, red, blue
from plastic bottles, they dab on
features—eyes and mouths.

And we would need legs as well,
one woman says,
as she smears herself a set.

The large head and little legs
look like a giant ovum
being admired by two sperm—

and this, also, is fundamental.
A man painting a landscape
squirts far too much yellow

on the paper, and says,
Let's just make the sun bigger.
And so, he does. My friend

Suzanne was like that.
Blind from Type 1 diabetes,
she always spoke

as if she could see,
as of course she could—
her own version, not

the darkness I expected.
On my way to the museum,
I walked across the Thames,

which was sleek and rippling,
like a muscled, oiled arm
reaching upriver to where

Suzanne used to live.
Frail as she was, she blazed
like a torched oil well with desires—

to ski down mountains,
to see her only child grow up.
The last time she called,

I didn't answer the phone
or call her back,
and you'd have to

chop off my head to rid me
of regret. Today, I press play
on the old machine

and she wishes me
a Happy Birthday again. Eyes
closed, I let her voice

wash over me. I love
the body, its ability
to endure, to keep

walking, walking,
even if the fierceness
is all in our heads.

Lines Written on a Loon's Skull

The way you consumed your prey—
death, too, gulped you whole,

broke you down
to constituent bones.

Your cranium—a tiny church
with a spinal hole I can whistle through.

Needle-nosed beak—how neatly
the lower jaw slots into,

and clutches, the upper,
like a 3-D puzzle piece.

Foramen—an opening, a pore,
a passage in bone—

under the arches guarding
your emptied eyes, a gibbous moon

stares back at me.
Are these pinprick holes where—

nerves, veins, arteries—you were
sewn together like a plush animal

and stuffed with life?
The elongate hollow in your upper beak—

is this the mournful place, the lake
where mist rises at dawn,

where you croon your call?
The life in you—

as I pencil these lines
on a tracing of your skull,

the letters are
tufts of sprouting feathers.

This poem has a highway in it

and it speeds upstate toward—
is it home if you've never lived there?
This poem merges, changes lanes, and exits—left, past the outlet mall,
then right. Mobile homes edge the road—and staggering barns.
Corn stubble pokes up through snow. A school bus brakes,

and a stop sign pops out. Two boys shuffle off, cross in front
of the poem and disappear. There's barbed wire
strung here. And a story. Stories, really. Three children
wrenched from their mother—dead, they're told, though
alive in an asylum they never find. The one sister, 17,

she drowns in a summer pond. There are purple hills, tall pines,
and silos in here, and field after field after field, forget about
dreams. Also a Dunkin' Donuts, grids of solar panels,
a Ford dealership. We're upstate, so a prison looms,
and rows of prison guards' pickups. Steam escaping

a prison chimney, a river running under a bridge. My mother's
in here, my stepfather, too—how he hugs women and girls
too close. As if asking: *are you my mother?* A shuttered restaurant
flies past, a motel without a car in the lot. The old armory
rises up, a red light against dusk, a left turn. The tumor

on my stepfather's neck and jaw fattens day after day—the consequence
of little mistakes. Six white horses commune around a mound of hay.
Fields offer up lone machinery: tractor, hay baler, mower, plow.
A dark blue silo. A burned-out house. Haloed by naked trees,
a neighbor's trailer blazes with light. There are humans

I love in this poem, a rearview mirror—the long, rutted driveway
glazed with ice and age. The house in this poem, a step up
from ramshackle, wasn't built all at once, but room by room.
Hundreds of acres, forests and fields. Two old bay horses, three ewes,
a hen and rooster, a border collie, a silver tabby. The humans in here

were children once. Things happened to them. They made
choices. This poem, too, makes choices, gets things wrong.
And some things can never be put right. But there's
mercy in here, tenderness. We cross in front of the poem,
we disappear—the poem goes on.

Thief

Only an animal with hands could have stolen the dish
of jelly I set out for the orioles last night. I picture

that Lone Ranger-faced raccoon up on its haunches
in the garden, lifting the orange-tinted glass bowl

to the August moon as it gulps down ShurFine
Concord grape. I forgive the thief. Who hasn't

been tempted by dark to steal something sweet?
But at the edge of the road, like a clump of hairy jelly,

lies a raccoon, stiff hands clutching at nothing. Sure,
maybe every delicious moment ends like this—

but fuck you anyway, truck or car—whatever you are.
Tonight, I'll raise a glass to what moon there is,

and lick up every last tongue-full of grief,
not because I'm a hero—because I'm a born thief.

Leave It

Like a wrecked ship, the white-ribbed
dead deer lists in the forest—

skull almost stripped, fur shedding
like snake skin, hooves askew
in ferns and last year's leaves—

dog-found—
flesh sniffed.

The archipelago of spine
trails off into small hips.
A black beetle

scrambles over the sacroiliac.
Other bugs—tiny black stealth bombers—

taxi along thigh bones.
A woodlouse wanders out
of a nostril onto the muzzle—

like patches of snow in spring,
how this last flesh clings.

Leave it, the deer says.

But we don't.

Notes

"Poetry Is Stolen Fruit" is indebted to Samuel Taylor Coleridge, Shakespeare, Supreme Court Justice Potter Stewart, Marianne Moore, Robert Frost, Matsuo Bashō, and Robert Hass.

"I Don't Want to Go Up in Smoke"—the quote is from *Beowulf: A New Verse Translation*, by Seamus Heaney (Farrar, Straus, and Giroux 1999).

"Dual Diagnosis" is after Agnar Artúvertin's poem "Eisini Tú" ("And You Too"), as translated from the Faroese by Matthew Landrum.

About the Author

Jennifer Stewart Miller was born in Massachusetts and grew up in Vermont and California. She holds an MFA from Bennington College, a JD from Columbia University, and a BA from Michigan State University, and is also the author of *A Fox Appears: A Biography of a Boy in Haiku* (2015) and a chapbook, *The Strangers Burial Ground* (Seven Kitchens Press 2020). Her poems have appeared in *Hayden's Ferry Review*, *Poet Lore*, *RHINO*, *Sugar House Review*, *Tar River Poetry*, and elsewhere. For more information, please visit JenniferStewartMiller.com.

Acknowledgments

Thank you to the following journals for first publishing versions of these poems:

Aquifer: The Florida Review Online: "Knees"

Cider Press Review: "To the Dead Striped Bass Swimming in Sunset" and "On Seeing"

Crab Creek Review: "Emerge" and "Poems I Probably Won't Write About My Stepfather"

Embers and Flames Anthology, ed. Whitney Scott, Outrider Press, June 2015: "Happy" and "Happy"

Heron Tree: "Under the Apple Tree"

Green Mountains Review Online: "Thirsty Birds" and "Baby Doc & the Green Crab"

Harpur Palate: "How to Convince Your Mother to Give Up the Farm"

The Jabberwock Review: "Thief" and "Because the pear tree"

The MacGuffin: "Due Date"

The National Poetry Review: "Walking Woman"

Peauxdunque Review: "Leave It"

Poet Lore: "Silversides"

Raleigh Review: "Dumped in swampy ground, axles up,"

Riddled with Arrows: "Poetry Is Stolen Fruit"

Rogue Agent Journal: "Cleaning the Night Basement"

Sugar House Review: "My Dead" and "This poem has a highway in it"

Sycamore Review: "Blizzard Aubade"

Tar River Poetry: "Lines Written on a Loon's Skull"

I am deeply grateful to Emily Mohn-Slate, Cassie Pruyn, Joanne Proulx, Denton Loving, Elaine Sexton, Marion Brown, and members of the 2 Horatio writing collective, who, in different ways, have helped me shape these poems and this manuscript—generous souls all.

Thank you also to my teachers at Bennington College Writing Seminars, April Bernard, David Daniel, Major Jackson, and Mark Wunderlich, for sharing their wisdom as well as advising me on some of the poems in this book. April Bernard deserves particular thanks.

Finally, where would I be without my wonderful family—Lindsay, Ryan, Chris, Lily, Scott, Anne Marie, Pam, Dolores, David, Jodi, Michael, Stephanie, Heidii, Rebecca, Greg, Gina, Alexi, Benji, my marvelous nieces and nephews…I am thankful for their love, support, and unique personalities.

CPSIA information can be obtained
at www.ICGtesting.com
Printed in the USA
BVHW030631280221
601323BV00013B/54